Waiting for Melody

Song Lyrics Without Music

By Izaak David Diggs

I don't write poems.

The following may seem like poems but they aren't, they are *song lyrics*. Semantics? No, they are sung to me by various singers I am into.

I hear music and someone singing the words to me, a line or two at a time.

It could be Greg Dulli's voice and music, it could be Dave Gahan of Depeche Mode, it could be Bob Dylan or Elvis Costello which is why this book is called *Waiting for Melody*; these are song lyrics to which--(aside from a few cases)--music has yet to be written.

No Words Come

No words come now
Only still lights
The cars and the crowds closing tight
The city's on guard says "you're alive"
Summer windows open
Lets the ocean sound freeway traffic in
The cars and the crowds even closer
World starts to spin

> No words come now
> Unable to move breath or speak
> No words come now
> Pulled too tight ready to break
> We're just running through the dark
> Looking for someone to hold us
> We're just running through the dark
> Fearing this life will be ripped from us

No words come now
There are no words for what you need to say
No words come now
The presence of light makes dreams go away
Did you see?
The world I let them throw at me
Did you see?
Them try to photograph the fear in me
Did you see?
The world I let them throw at me?
Did you see?
The midnight cars, lost and far, adrift in the city...

Cellophane <3

Cellophane heart
Melting in a world of smoke
Spread out like tea leaves in the dark
Your dreams sweep from tragedy to farce
Somebody tell me
How to get there
The world is on fire
And strangers stole the chairs

Cellophane heart
Stretched too thin
The sky turned to water
And the water turned to gin
Somebody tell me
Because every breath is a mystery
The world tastes like smoke
And the weather leaves riddles in the tops of the trees

Cellophane heart
The world loves to watch you
Fall down the stairs
The blind love it when you're bare
Somebody open the drapes
Because in the dark I'm only half awake
Come close to the window
There is a sky to judge, pills to take
Come close to the window
And see a world where angels break

Camphor

Remember when I used to get under your skin?
And you got under mine
Leave the bathroom door open
And I'll spill all your wine
Now I'm many many days less young
My skin is getting too red
I can't brush the dust off my shoes
And I keep falling out of bed

The world is full of knives
But I haven't any fear
They can penetrate my skin
But I left my blood in another year
Sometime in the past
When I felt love and bled like a normal man
You might recall that person
Someone I no longer am

You used to say I left you itching
Well, I recall you pawing at your limbs
Turning scratches into wounds
As I watched from across the room
There's not a big enough desert
To swallow the memory of the rain
There's not enough camphor in the world
For certain types of pain

The world is full of knives (etc.)

All These STARS Collide

Death is not the end
Just the end of the beginning
You're pulling on a string
And the theory is weary
The physics of weakness
Won you a nobel prize
Maybe the day you'll wake up
Is the day you die
And all these stars collide

Your imaginary friend
Does all the talking
He's the better dressed one
With the Facebook following
The adverice of your cologne
Advertises a slapdash disguise
It's funny how you look when you're laughing
The same as when you cry

Someday you'll feel
The love Christ has for you
It'll follow you around the room
Like the eyes in a creepy painting
But in a good way
Like the warm endless embrace
Of someone you love
Too too far away
Maybe you knew me
Before I learned it's best to hide
Maybe you thought you knew me
Maybe you dreamed up my better side
But my love that part of me has died
And all these stars collide

Another   Tourist   in   Hell

You were a good girl
Too good for me
A dirty face in the crowd
What did you see?
I am hurt and disgrace
Gnarled up like nightmare sheets
Curdled with sweat like feverish thoughts
You had nothing but love for me
And I had no dream but to watch you bleed

I am a curse on two legs
Unworthy of any praise or redemption
You came scratching at my door
I betrayed you without hesitation
I am a idea for murder
Scratched on a balled up napkin
Look in my cold, disgraced eyes
I am too shamed for this world

You came rubbing against me
I could pet you, then stab you in the spine
Now I imagine you writhing
It cuts through my thoughts time after time
I may be a thief
But I am no Robin Hood
I am a fucked up cruel seducer
Who will come to no good
I contemplate your murder
Not by my hand, but just as well
I am tormented by every second of your pain
Another tourist in hell

Back Rooms of Your Mind

The lights build like cities in my mind
I need you to get closer
But it's stay away time
I turn on the radio to open the door
She walks in sits on the edge of the bed
Going in and out of key
As She sings along with voices in my head

There could have been so much
Chose the window instead of the door
There could have been so much
But you just got older
There could have been so much
Now there's just a history of wasting time
There could have been so much
But you chose to live in the back rooms of your mind

The night builds in typical desperation
We're running away
With no idea of destination
I send Her every form of correspondence
Waiting for a reply
Does She still have the memory
Going in and out of key
As She sings along with the voices in my head

I've been feeling weak, feeling shaky
Like it's the onset of the end
Everything falling in on me
Still expected to pretend
I know why She left me to feel this way
Left me without an answer
She left me singing to myself
In the key of disaster

Choir

He was a choir boy and she watched him
Drift across the the grounds like a melody
She thought, I could stain your lips with mine
I would let you find me
I want nothing more than to get so lost
A tourist in your city

      Somewhere there is love for you
      Somewhere there is a warm embrace
      Somewhere no one will ever leave you
      Somewhere they will accept you
      And how I want to be there with you

These ever shortening days
Don't remain long enough to learn their names
Every hurt becomes an ache
And you allow each one to burn you like a flame
She finds herself watching him again
I see your shape through your clothes
See the color of your skin
Another secret no one can know

      Somewhere there is love for you (etc.)

We share these nights
Look into each other's eyes
But you see one thing
And I see another
She had to walk away
Before everything became insane
Close her heart like a gate
With too many locks, too many breaks

      Somewhere there is love for you (etc.)

Cornered

Ugliness writes itself on my skin
Again, it should be a sin
But it's all this disgust manifesting
Toe on the trigger pull the pin
Pretend you understand this friend
The good Lord will make you bleed for what you said
It's the good Lord I need, but I feel alone again

       Lies lies goodbye
       No more excuses time to die
       No point in breathing, nothing left to try
       All this stupid pride
       And only that to show, with no place left to go
       Cornered

You ask me if I can change
It's strange, but I don't feel deranged
But deception is in my character
I cannot wear this fucking mask anymore
I cannot live with this weight in my heart anymore
The song changes key, it's time to flee
When you change your tune
It's like waking up in a stranger's bed
When you change your tune
It's like waking up in a stranger's head
The good Lord will make you bleed for what you said
It's the good Lord I need, but I feel alone again

       Lies lies goodbye
       No more excuses time to die
       No point in breathing, nothing left to try
       All this stupid pride
       And only that to show, with no place left to go
       Cornered

The street light is flickering
My cells are trembling
Soon the shadows will be casting
Me in the starring role, I am cornered

DAYLIGHT

Wait until the next day
Wait until the next time you wake
Something you had to say
To fill the tension a silence makes
But my skin feels like a prison
My head is full of madness
There seems no hope at all now
I'm getting drunk on the sadness

Wait until the daylight
Is it necessary to be cheerful and fake?
Wait until the daylight
I needed that last drink
Now it sends a smug telegram
A twist in the patent of all my plans
A voice that simmers with glee
Its tones will be the death of me

So, I waited for the daylight
I put your picture in a suitcase
But I still feel the snapshot in my hands
Just another lost headcase
I never meant for things to go this way
But you had to dance
To music I cannot stand
It's an unspeakable circumstance
Somewhere, we share the daylight
You watch the sunrise through a sheen of pain
Saying another stupid prayer
That a fool like me will love you again

DESERT   NIGHTS

Take the broken road to the lower parts of town
Where a fear of sleep weighs us down
Murder in the air that seductively surrounds
This celebration, sing the songs of children
As the saints incorporate their lies
All their smiles have been televised
As their intentions creep like eyes
Up your skirt and past your thighs

You will poison yourself again
In the desert nights, in the desert nights
You were looking for a friend
In the desert nights, in the desert nights
You will imprison yourself again
In the desert nights, in the desert nights
Looking for the beginning of the end
In the desert nights, in the desert nights

You were just a pair of tits in a magazine
And I was the devil or at least a facsimile
The assassination will cross your coat to be
Like a touch of dissonance in the harmony
They forced all of us fools to sing
Without the rhythm or meter to swing
Finding a way to invent a time machine
To go back and invent your enemies

You will poison yourself again
In the desert nights, in the desert nights
You were looking for a friend
In the desert nights, in the desert nights
You will imprison yourself again
In the desert nights, in the desert nights
Looking for the beginning of the end
In the desert nights, in the desert nights

I Will Not Destroy You

I wish I knew how to love you, but I do not
My love is strong but astray for you
Running too cold, running too hot
I will banish you before I betray you
I will send you down a darkening road
I will break my own heart in two
Maybe I was born to hurt you
I only hope this does not destroy you

I've got blood underneath my nails, my dear
It tastes like the secret streets of your heart
Footprints of your blood in my soul
I've got your blood like pained art
And I keep drawing from that last moment
Your eyes rose to meet mine
You looked so scared, so confused
I wish you would never trust again
but you will

I wish I knew how to love you, but I do not
My love for you is true but pointedly askew
At this moment I wish I were the coldest person alive
But a part of me zeroes in on you
You reach from the past and I am crucified
I used to hold you like a child
You ran to the window when I came by
I said I will not destroy you
But despite all we wanted that became a lie...

Let Me **Hide**

A heart is a house of horrors
Each beat a shadow of itself
Coming on with a smile
Like a traitor in all its stealth
Coming on like a lover
With murder in his belt
The anger is an angel
Rising on this soft, unmentioned beauty
Spreading a soft scent like home
Then exploding into fury
You want me to stand out in the open
Just let me hide
You want me to face the light of day
Just let me hide
I cannot describe the disgust I feel
Just let me hide
I cannot stand anything inside
Just let me hide

A heart is a stupid machine
Full of clanks
Blowing out sickly sweet steam
Looking for thanks
After it blows up like a bad dream
Full of contrary faces
That brew in your conscious like alcohol
I may seem to be sitting still
As I plot to climb over the wall...
You want me to stand out in the open (etc.)

Love Ya

Who came into the room?
Big smile for the crowd
Who can hold a secret--
while talking so loud?
Another baby in the dumpster
Launch a new life
Blowing kisses, love ya
Another BFF to forget tomorrow
Miss the joke, miss the boat
No more bad feelings, love ya

Who knows the right words?
The comforting grin, new best friend
Is the day half gone? Inner animatron
Who loves ya baby?
The boy still looks for you
Love ya, another baby in the dumpster
Maybe the boy still needs you
But reaching out has no dividend
High five a stranger, new best friend
Love ya, love ya, love ya

Only the Foolish

There's a girl in the room
She's too thin for breathing
Soon all the memories will gather
To set the twilight reeling
Tell the men in the coats to take back their bad
Our kisses a tight leash in your hand
Our skin stained with yesterday
You grew your hair it's another year

There's a girl in the room
Fading lines on yellowing paper
All your little fools gather
Swimming through your ego like remnants of ether
We're riding on the backs
Of giants with our eyes closed
There's a disaster brewing in your veins
Like a melody only the foolish know...

The Cha Cha Man

The cha cha man
Reading the dusty crowd
Like a surgeon reads a wound
Curing you of life itself
The parlor tricks come shyly
Holds your dreams for ransom
Like a soft spoken child
Born to be an assassin

All the lairs needed a king
Someone to rule the mud
Like a fever in the brain
Or a derangement of the blood
The cheap hello
That creeps up like a virus
Watch him pitch like a ship
And you'll never see home again

In the middle of the night
He escapes to your room
To measure your breathing
The rapture of your skin
Crooked yellow smile
Like hasty tombstones
Promising to hold your hand
After your heart stills...

THE NEVERMAKER

A dream is a funny thing
Wearing each day like a see through shirt
Uncomfortable but vain
Missteps so fashionably hurt
Could you ever love a bad man like me?
I am a nevermaker
The rusty smile of a bear trap
I'm the pulse in a panic

    It's not fashionable
    To be intelligent so
    You'll always be in style
    All your little fools gather
    I may be a nevermaker
    But I will never be trapped
    In the adverice of your cologne

Every heart has a rhythm
All music has basis in math
Your watching for calculation
When my hand is on your calf
A dream is a funny thing, mine keep me awake
A madman's car with the windows down
An unmapped street in a sleepy town

    It's easy to follow the crowd
    A middle aged woman from Queens
    With a goiter and photographer dreams
    Captures your march into a ravine
    Like doll parts fed into a machine
    And you all come out the same

I am a nevermaker, I don't make eye contact
I can refrain from speaking
I can pretend I don't need anyone
And on the subject of lying, I know exactly what I'm doing
Every breath has a purpose, every sharp retort is a tourniquet
When I feel my strength fading away, I know exactly when I'm doing
I will stand when I feel like sitting, I will open myself to the whole plan
And wonder if you could ever love a bad man, like me

Ugly Boots

It's the beginning of the whether
When your sugar sours
In another town hope cowers
Chalking up your bell jar hours
Why bother getting out of bed?
When there's a car crash in your head
All the victories have been bled
The director sets another scene

Polish your ugly boots
coffee stains on a pinprick suit
Wait til the sugar returns sweet
And the days glisten with sweat
A calibration to this cowardice
All the things we have to miss
Tidy the bell jar this hopeful mess
The director sets another scene

We All Go Down to the Shore (the Beach Boys song that never was)

I used to have faith, but I don't anymore
I used to follow the road to the city
Now I just lie on the floor

I used to call out to you, hopeful with the voice of a child
I used to sleep all night long until the world grew brutal careless and wild
(The sirens, the sirens, the sirens, the danger)

I used to go down to the sea marvel at the currents
I used to go down to the sea wonder what it all meant
Now I fear the tides and my desire to throw myself in
I've spent my life looking for places to hide in a game I can't possibly win
(the sirens, the sirens, the sirens, the danger)

We all go down to the shore when the sun is strong
Searching for good times when the days are long

We all go down to the shore, pavement hot as embers
We all go down to the shore fall down and surrender
(the sirens the sirens the sirens the danger)
 Your reflection on the semi-still water looks lovely tonight (4X)

Maybe we'll get lost in this big crazy city pinned in chaos drift away
And if we die in this crazy city it'll be okay

When We Wuz Gangsta

You and I are strays
Never meant to call anywhere home
Locking ourselves out from love
Stationed out alone

A star falls, a heart burst
Words are forgotten ammunition
Living just gets worse
Pain beyond imagination
So we cling to those memories
When we wuz gangsta, ruling the empty
streets
Wearing a crown of alcohol
That melted at our feet
In our velour tracksuits
Posing so strong, so proud
Before it got to be too much
Before life broke us down

You and I are strays
And we never will belong
Speaking another language
Everything inside is wrong
Long ago we spun like planets
On meaningless strips of cardboard
We posed like paper mache Tupacs
Before we fell on our swords

Remember when we wuz gangsta
That feeling nothing could stop us

In our stupid naive convictions
We had this unwavering trust
But now it's all gone
No reason to go on
It was all just a fantasy
Now it's all just bad dreams on repeat
Every smile has a pull back
Forced like a knife to the neck
Or the slow death of your heart
As you lie there in the dark
Begging for sleep...

when we wuz gangsta

Black Ruby

All hope is nearly gone
The lie inside my mind has died
Things we know are wrong
Last resorts time to cross a line
You don't care how close I am
You ignore how dire it's become
You have no idea how close I am
You keep talking, but not listening
          All strength is nearly gone
          Nearly out of my mind I'm fucked up this time
          All reason is nearly gone
          To protect you from the ultimate mercy
          All optimism soon will be gone
          My heart is crushed and gasping
          All hope is nearly gone, my heart is a black ruby
Frustration, salvation, close your eyes, open the window
Frustration, salvation, close your eyes, here we go
Frustration, salvation, you know it's time, time to go
Frustration, salvation, I will leave no mark, leave no shadow
          All hope is nearly gone
          The lie inside my mind has died
          Things we know are wrong
          Last resorts time to cross a line
          It's become too much to bear
          I have to think for myself and I won't be spared
          It's become too much to bear
          It's gotten to be too much, too much
All strength is nearly gone
Nearly out of my mind I'm fucked up this time
All reason is nearly gone
To protect you from the ultimate mercy
All optimism soon will be gone
My heart is crushed and gasping
All hope is nearly gone, my heart is a black ruby

I have ruined everything, I made the mistake of believing
I have ruined everything by believing in myself
Frustration, salvation, close your eyes, open the window (etc.)

BLACK

RUBY

Broke Down in Tucson

Don't leave me staring at the sky
Whiling away another threadbare night
Don't leave me longing for your table
Permeating my skin smooth as sable
Don't leave me anticipating
You're waiting round the bend
Don't leave me broke down
Broke down in Tucson again

Don't leave me with stories
No one will believe
Of being touched in a way
No mere mortal can conceive
Don't drag me through an oasis
Then leave me in the desert
Don't leave me anticipating
You're waiting round the bend
Don't leave me broke down
Broke down in Tucson again

Do you feel as compelled?
Or did you use me?
To satisfy your needs
To satisfy your curiosity?
Broken too many times
A heart will never mend
And I will never find my way
Since you left me broke down
Broke down in Tucson again

Cruel Suggestion

You walked across the room, all cruelty and beauty
Your perfume coded and strong
Your smile secretive but easy
Making me see a side of myself
I should never have found
You spoke of a beauty that exists
When no one else is around
And I let all your lies into my bloodstream
Let it rush under my skin and reshape me

      You saw I was vulnerable
      And told me of an amazing place
      Where everything makes sense
      Loving were the lies recited to my face
      And now there is no hope
      There's nothing left but depression
      You showed me a life with meaning
      But it was just a cruel suggestion

There was this amazing promise
And you brought it into the air
But like a magician trained in malice
Or a thief gifted with smoke and mirrors
You whispered of a greatness
I would not be allowed to achieve
And now everything joyous and worthwhile
Is dissolving inside me

      You saw I was vulnerable (etc.)

So, is this your entertainment?
A capricious, ragged game?
Listening for the last rupture of my heart
As I struggle through another day
I thought I saw a promise
Some warmth even love in your eyes
As you showed me a side of myself
I would come to despise...

Curse the Water

Feels so cool going down
Burns from the inside out
Takes away all the disgust
Leaves you writhing on the ground
Tends to be complicated
Things that seemed so clear
Leads me to seek an exit
Leads me to gin, leads me to beer
It's so easy to curse the water
So easy to embrace
I could drink til I drown
Even when I don't care for the taste
So boring to stand upright
I'd rather fall on my face

I just play the game
I just do as I'm told
And it feels like a fucking waste
And I'm getting dangerously parched
Every day there's resentment and pain
Everyday feels just a little bit longer
But you say curse the water
Every day feels just a little bit longer
But you say curse the water

The disgust gets immeasurable
Like a sea designing to swallow ships
And spit back the legends
That only roll from fearful lips
As much as I care for you
I will not be your martyr
So keep that in mind
Every time you tell me to curse the water
Keep all this in mind
When you tell me to curse the water...

Drowning in **Delight**

Before you learned to drown
Your grace was solemn profound
Then came the weight that gave you shadow and restraint
Months of quicksand self-assurance
Rising like bees from a broken hive
Language learns to sting when it comes alive
The sea turned deep when we dared to dive
Diving into deep delight

Deep like love or madness
Nuanced like pain or wisdom's riddle
The stars made patterns like drunken conversation
Like a car you swerved into accidental revelation
Ice on the wings meant to carry you high
Are you really rising when you start to dive?
Are you really living or is this what it means to die
When you dive into deeper delight

Tell me, is the house still standing?
Tell me, love, when will my heart stop breaking?
I made this offhand character strong
But I heard the direction all wrong
I fear the end of every night
When daybreak brings a scourge to my sight
And the devil kisses me like tides rising
Soon I fall further, further from your sight
As I drown in deeper delight…

Even if You Run

Now that you're a statistic
Do you reflect on an impulse
And bitterly regret it?
Wishing you could retract it
Faster than a speeding bullet
Or a drink supposed to be nursed
I was the older one
I was supposed to go FIRST

Now I get to live with this
Although we both get to pay
Hits me like a punch drunk marathoner
When I begin to feel okay
Don't let the door hit your ass
When you're too impatient to say goodbye
It's harder to trust a friend
Than to give up and die

This is one of the bad days
When nothing can be won
The tighter I pull it together
I still feel completely undone
Right now I want to throttle you
Unleash every obscenity under the sun
But at the heart of it
I'll still love you EVEN if you run
I wish I could have given you solace
But what's done is done
Even if you grow small in the distance
I'll still love you EVEN if you run...

Hit Me

There's a beautiful girl
With bones in her eyes
With two kids in the car
And one on the way
There's a letter of apology
Getting dirty on the floor
There's his smells on the clothes
He won't be wearing any more

> She sits in the kitchen, and no one can help her
> Just the check for two hundred
> Sent by her mother
> Creditors call from 8 to 8, she listens helplessly
> To their echo as she tries to sleep
> Fearing the things she'll see

Four years ago there were dreams
You're young and open, feeling you can do anything
Til the first hurt gets under your skin
All you can do is cry air, your face twisted and red
Looking at a life that seems dead
Like the one who shared your life, your bed
Hit me, cut me, wound me
I feel absolutely nothing now
Hit me, cut me, wound me
My heart is an abbey; all prayers have been abandoned

> His uniform is in the closet, she just stares at the door
> Another call for the mastercard, another from the landlord
> One of the kids is crying, but she can't make herself move
> Fearing all the knives she keeps behind the stove

Four years ago there were dreams (etc.)

Holy Shit

vodka yoga
call me when you don't know better
I know every excuse
Down to each letter
I'm a child
And I've lost my keys again
I'm a man
With a will too strong to bend
(self) preservation
(self) destruction
(self) preservation
(self) destruction
(self) preservation
(self) destruction
your breath moves like anger
down my skin
I'm hard and moving through
Rooms so out of tune
Things in my heart
I'm sure you don't want to know
As I gild your precious lives
Like poetry from a wino
(self) preservation,(self) destruction
(self) preservation,(self) destruction
(self) preservation,(self) destruction
So purposefully
You'll seek the things that bring
A momentary glee
A momentary gleam
But listen to me
You're turning a bend my friend
Closer to the me
That is a measure from the meaning...

Sky High

You left death like present
Outside an unlocked door
Left all these dreams crucified
Like a false jesus waiting for more
The anticipation of such a gift
Another purposeless lie
Left us weightless useless
Waiting to drift sky high

So, I will lose any sense of worth
I will rend my skin
Examine the blackness
Wait until the end
So say your fucking farewells
While you still have a chance
Before I cheat gravity one last time
And you can watch me...
Sky high

I have wasted enough of your time
I have led you astray
Believing in impossible things
That never had a chance
Life is too cruel for that
So turn off all the pilots
Let it drift towards our peace
Now you've found your perfect match
It's time to understand release
I've just had this foolish idea
A beautiful corruption in my head
That I would be worth more to you
If I were
Sky high...

Taut Goes the Murder Wire

This love breeds beneath your skin
In rhythm, like horses swim
My heart held together by rusty wires and confusion
Colors like a lovers sunfall or a contusion
An execution, a beautiful child beams
Skipping down the street, a totalitarian regime
Kittens and whiskey, green streams and gasoline
Suicide letters revealed in moonbeams
I'm optimistic starting to tire
Taut goes the murder wire

I want to live, I don't want to
I want to live I don't want to

A boundless love, a sleepless night
Cruel thoughts drive these earthly delights
You know I'd give my life for you
You know often I go on living just for you
Where dreams evolve when dreams expire
Taut goes the murder wire
The mother that believes you
The father that leaves you
The stirrings that are faithful
The hope that is deceitful
Though my heart breaks a little more
The beating grows stronger
Eternal cities rise, frail dreams are sired
Taut goes the murder wire

Come a little closer, keep your distance...

Memories Burn Like Stars

It was July when you wrote out the rules
Kisses do flare and love is for fools
That purple shirt did raise your voice
But not the feelings you'd skillfully avoid
You had to smile, I was a child in some regards
Sometimes innocence has its rewards
Love is weakness to be murdered in bars
All your memories burn like stars

I wrote those words in the last century
Back when language had its sting
You had a cavalier way with a simple dress
My lack of education caused you distress
We were beautiful together for awhile
But crushes fade like motors dissolve miles
My name in your memory is too deep to jar
Yet all your memories burn like stars

It's easy to give your life when you know you'll never die
It's easy to give your heart suspecting you'll never cry
It's easy to age when being young means nothing
And reading your diary is like analyzing handwriting
You looked through a door I thought would never close
But often ignorance is based on what little we actually know
Now your just three songs and some memory in a car
But all those memories burn like stars
You looked through a door I thought would never close

But often ignorance is based on what little we actually know
Now your just three songs and some memory in a car
But all those **memories burn like stars**...

Gash

Do you remember that dance we did?
memory is like a disease
the snow was hard and white as doves
and we crawled it on our knees
Just to see
Just to feel the brightness of the sky sear our eyes
Just to see
Just to be, just to see
Just to steal one more moment

The weather is crazy like 3 am laughter
It's time to shiver
You collect your cash the hurt leaves a gash
That you framed take the blame
It took a martyr to give it a name
So bend, til you're black and blue
Lost the beat between three and two
So cut, skin doesn't mean a thing
So cut, it'll go deeper than you think

Do you remember that mask you wore?
Keep those memories on a leash
the rain was sharp and cool as shards
and we crawled in on our knees
Just to see
Just to feel the brightness of the sky sear our eyes
Just to see
Just to be, just to see
Just to steal one more moment
The weather is crazy like 3 am laughter
It's time to shiver…

Bleed it Like a Stone

Remember that air you breathed?
Were you deceived it'd keep coming
Remember the gash on your arm
Self harm, it's so charming
So pursued, the flat-line afternoons
You thought there'd be someone to love you
But you were just some meat to be chewed
Torn to bits but never consumed

Bring on the ghost that you chose
In poorly chosen clothes we'll step on your toes
We'll squeeze the water from the mud
So bleed it like a stone
Bring on the ghost that you chose
In poorly chosen clothes we'll step on your toes
Steal the copper scent from your blood
So bleed it like a stone...

Wave(JBS)

"I'm just riding my wave
And the ocean, is so gray
Cold surges of water
Close to carrying me away"
Knew when you said that
There was a reason to be scared
Turned around when I heard the door
Turned back and you weren't there

"I'm just riding my wave
You think that you know me
But you only know my name
Riding my wave
Yes, I'll pull on that face
And yes
You'll see me everyplace
But I'll be gone
Riding my wave
I'm just riding my wave
And it hurts too much
More than I can say"
       While everybody slept
       You went to the sea all alone
       It was incredibly peaceful
       Though the air chilled you to the bone
       Didn't fear getting carried off
       To lands never mapped
       Didn't fear getting carried off
       You were too tired for that
       And you were riding your wave
       Riding your wave...

Ghost on the subway

The beautiful sting of a stolen kiss
Brought me from my worst
Held you so close I could breathe for you
Who'll open their eyes first?
Meet you in the bathroom, dear
Pulling at the hem of your dirty shirt
Looking for words in the mirror
Holding everything in til it hurts

Was it the beginning of something?
Cause everything you said haunted me
As I lay in bed alone
Trying to find our past on my phone
Drifting like a ghost on the subway
Collecting like smoke on a train
Every face a reminder
Every station looking the same

She came ornately fifteen minutes late
And twenty minutes later I was resigned to my fate
Too much drunken laughter over the phone
A beautiful girl waiting for the snow
It gets too cold outside
Everything and everyone can seem insane
Much better to lie together in the dark
Watching the shadows change, listen to the rain

Took her hand on a desolate street
Her skin cool as the window next to my bed
The rhythm of her blood sane in a winter world
Drowning out the doubt in my head

Gleaming Glass Doors

It takes the architect of failure
To build on a dying conversation
I know when to shut up, when intent is beyond articulation
It's easy to feel corrupt
When the sand shows you what's inside
Dark shapes in the looking glass make you so nervous you have to laugh

Take a little pill to level you out
Take a little drink to steady your hands
Take a little step through the gleaming glass doors
Your little steps echoing on the cool floor
The smell of flowers you cannot name
The cut of feelings you cannot tame
You and I will die one day, until that moment we play this game

In our private films we're dictator
Fronting a semi neurotic regime
Standing proud with a hand in our vests
While feeling self-conscious of the seems
It's easy to feel unloved, when you put too much on being needed
It's easy to feel unknown, when you choose to spend your life on your knees
Take a little pill to level you out (etc.)

Some skim along the surface, some are stupid enough to dive
Some understand what we perceive is the truth
Is subjective, as subjective as a variation on a lie
I will let this course through me a moment more
As your last letter reads like a suicide note
Waving as you walk through those gleaming glass doors
As these words die in my throat

The lights are lower now
It's late and the air is uncertain

Staring into the empty intersections
A still lowering like a curtain
Your smile changes with the minutes
Another disguise to chafe
The glasses are too close together
Catching the light like a gift of disgrace

Some days it's easier to bleed
But we learn to hide our skin
Some days it's easier to need
Something, but you learn to pretend
I will lie to your face
Because we both know it's better that way
When I tell you everything is okay
And make a gift of disgrace

You can make harmony of dissonance
Sometimes angels smile through gritted teeth
Cutting the air with a violence
So beautiful, like a ship making love to a reef
Somedays break like bones
Somedays end like innocence
Somedays bathe you in soft light
Somedays burn a secret in your heart...

Gleaming
Glass
Doors

Wreak That Ship

Was it delight by design?
Death by deduction
Your hard line face is like a map now
Your scoured emotions coming nude
Sour goes the new day
Sour glides through our weary blood
Sour goes the new day
Wreak that ship see how far is down
Wreak that ship see how far is down

There is nowhere to land
The compass fell out of your hand
Is that a wall of gray on the horizon?
Is that our clock ticking down?
Is that a wall of gray on the horizon
There's no hope for us now

There's architecture in murder
Straight lines in destruction
Your hard line face is unyielding
Like some long dead genius cut you from stone
Sour goes the new day
Sour glides through our jittery blood
Sour goes the new day
You have a reason to be afraid
Wreak that ship see how far is down
Wreak that ship see how far is down

There is nowhere to land (etc.)

Dying Like Gene Vincent on a Stranger's Veranda

Shit stacks on shit stacks on shit
Little monkey makes piles, little monkey makes piles
Shit stacks on shit stacks on shit
Little monkey makes piles, makes piles of money
Little monkey
Little monkey

Cripple in black leather he leans
Likes a fedora, sweat comes down in streams
Now you bend when you walk
Well now, you sound bent when you talk
Careening so cool you're a motorcycle crash
Burning like the startle that ices your blood

Shit stacks on shit stacks on shit (etc.)

One day you will not be so strong so sure
One day you will find yourself vulnerable
One day you will feel impossibly small and scared
One day you might just end up human
Breathing gets harder have to stand up
Being alive goes from automatic to math
Just like the late great Gene Vincent
Went from flesh and blood to a worn photograph...

Blood Moves Like Sugar

Another day passes
Numbly staring into space
You could walk through a million people
Not recognize a single face
We pick up on fear
Like splinters seek our skin
The love of anonymous injury
Some loves come too easily
Your blood moves like sugar
Rushing like some strange music
Only you and I can hear
Night falls the melody changes
You walk faster but hope strides out of range

Everything feels out of date
Like a waiting room magazine
Everyone tells you to be strong
No one ever tells you how to be weak
People tell you how to live
No one ever tells you how to die
I recognize that light shining in my eyes
Won't bother feinting surprise
These things move slow
Like blood in our weary veins
Some people always called us vain
But for you and I there was never any other way
You drew a map on my arm
In black magic marker
The ink got in my blood flowed to my heart
And I've been lost ever since...

We Live Underwater

Lost as we may be
Hand in hand in injury
The way your pale skin catches the light
The way we wait until the safety of night
Close your eyes
Blood still circulates
These kisses burn in slow motion
We learn to hesitate

Did you write another name
On the card you sent back home?
Does that word mean anything?
Just another place to be leaving
You raise a madness in my blood
I close my eyes and let it breed
You're so delicately strong
And you and I will never belong

We live underwater
Currents move us in circles
Our beauty is unwritten
And our dreams will not be forgiven
For leaving us in a town where we cannot speak
For leaving us with truths we can't believe
For leaving us bound to our fears
For leaving me without you all these years...

burn smolder BURN

burn smolder burn
bruise cut bruise
burn smolder burn
bruise cut bruise

Your skin is the place that you hide
Your sin is to think of names for what you feel
You sink into thoughts too deep for the stone
That falls into cold currents too dark to gauge
It's a given you'll come to the last page
Of another over-rated book you swore you'd set down

burn smolder burn (etc.)

Your skin is a map of injuries
Written in expressions and in scars
You swore that drink would be your last
But you ignore the hours like the last man in a bar
This dream of peace is a mask
You slip on your face as if joining a cast
Of actors way beyond your sage
And you make up a new character as you fall off the stage
Watch you, burn smolder burn
See you, burn smolder burn
Hear you, burn smolder burn
Sense you, burn smolder burn
You made yourself forgettable, see
Saw what you want unforgivable
The river is rising like a curious gaze
And you will be cold like black, still water the rest of your days
The river is rising like a curious gaze
And you will be cold like dark still water the rest of your days...

Peppy Cando and the Smile Machine

So, wipe the eyes off the front of your pretty, summer dress
And give some charm to the lies on the cue cards as
Tiny faced men engage in hasty masturbation
The world is standing by with temporary fascination
Another food trend, another break out star
Who will be working in a Wal Mart in less than two years
Don't you want to kiss the world as you stab it in the heart?
As darkness kisses the back of your gorgeous, toned neck
Those things that couldn't touch you somehow left a mark
As we wait for your smile machine to shudder to a stop

God gives little girls like you the beauty to destroy
God gives little boys like us this churning bestial lust
God gives us desire, but not so much instruction
God gives us desires, and they lead to our destruction
Tell us of unspeakable train wreaks and drownings
With that lovely smile you wear
Tell us of children dying and cities burning
And who does your hair you really must share
The camera really loves you, just don't go too deep
The camera really loves you
But tomorrow it'll murder you in your sleep...

DEPRESSION ERA LOVE STORY

Clutching at your skin the show begins to start
Hard light and dust and this weight in our hearts
No one warned us away from all the pain
Of the breath to breath and day to day
Do we really belong here? Is this the life we're meant to?
Weight face breadline stare, we had dreams but did we dare to
Believe there could be something better for you and I?
Then counting breaths and prayers until the day we die
How can your smile still be so innocent?
When I see the subtext of your every half-smiled aside?
We see the dust on our shoes and feel ashamed
A clock runs a little slower across the room...

AMBIDEXTROUS GLOVE

You move in so easy
Like a bathwater baby
Maybe no one knows your name
Being unknown becomes a game
And one you race like a train
Dominating landscapes

And it can go any way, you say
Do what you decide and go for a ride
And it can go any way, you say
Do what you decide and go for a ride

Cancel the night I'm afraid of the lights
And the lie that has become our living
You can choose to make an art of pain
Dominating landscapes

And it can go any way, you say (etc.)

Swimming beneath the bridge
You change the meaning of water
Try it again on the other hand
Swimming beneath the bridge
Like an island with a pulse
You're a trick just like quicksand

And it can go any way, you say (etc.)

Beige

Soundbite disconnect
Gloss it up make it pretty
Power windows big smile time
Air conditioned for your tune out
Hide in your big house
Beige with paper walls
Close enough to eavesdrop
Your neighbors know your habits
But don't know your name
> We're filming our own reality show
> Standing still we're on the go
> Waiting for the death blow
> Below there's nothing but soothing static
> Take a pretty pill to smooth the rage
> Haven't had a thought for days
> Somebody take this hurt away
> Everything is beige
Smooth talk gestapo walk
Extreme power drink fame ranger
Your latest super phone
So three and a half minutes ago
Super size the bullshit
Gates around the community
Gates around a prison
> We're filming our own reality show (etc.)
The emptiness inside is wide
And weaving a vast that'll always last
Every breath is like broken glass
Twisting in your nerves
Did I be and say the right thing?
Guess not because you're running away
Lost track wore the wrong mask
Absolutely nothing is made to last

Missed Phone Call

If I ever hear your voice again
I'll be grateful until the end
Of my life
We make ghosts out of lovers and friends
Instead of climbing we choose to descend
Out of spite

I am so sorry I wasn't there
It will haunt me until I die
I am so sorry I wasn't there
And sorry is as meaningless as saying goodbye

Will you ever let yourself see
How I loved you completely?
To the point of absurdity
A heart shaped calamity
The memory of your face is all that I know
When I'm scared with nowhere to go
When my emotions are in a war they can't possibly win
Adrift on an ocean of whiskey and gin

People look for the meaning of life
Chances are there isn't one at all
We're just a collection of accidents
A series of missed phone calls
We all know pain will track us down
But life's too short for introspection
We like to pretend we're happy being lost
Because we fear our destination…

Roads Converge Roads Di-verge
(sung to me by Van Morrison in the middle of the night)

What are you doing in there? What you got in there?
Roads converge and roads diverge
Over peaks through shadowed valleys
What you doing in there? What you got in there?
Roads converge and roads diverge
Around towns where saints fell in their blood
Love collapsed and rose and nights misunderstood
What you doing in there? What you got in there?
Truths murdered, walls came up fell down
And I was too sure of myself, someone accidentally found
Roads converge and roads diverge
People tried to learn names that fell off their tongues
They cried in crowds and only smiled when surrounded by no one
What you doing in there? What you got in there?
Oh, the sheets were in twists like waves too angry to embrace the beach
Oh, there was no money just pebbled ceilings where the spiders die observing
Roads converge and roads diverge
We were huddled in the darkness
The chill painting clouds on the windows
Collecting like rain where the street gets low
What you doing in there? What you got in there?
Death rode by but we were too young to care
Roads converge and roads diverge….

The Pathologist

Anaphylactic shock GMO crops
Celebrity news and murderous cops

The bees sting us into another season, the bees sting is into another year.

You know it's love when I'm watching you
You act scared but I know you like it too
I've seen under your skin
I know where life begins
You know it's love when I'm watching you
You act scared but I know you like it too
I've seen under your skin
I know how life ends

The bees sting us into another season, the bees sting us into another year.

How I love you lying there
Silent stare seeing nothing
How I love you lying there
I'm the only one who knows you

The bees sting us into another season, the bees sting us into another year....

May I Please Tug at Your Hem

May I paint myself
In a corner of your room
May I be a bird on your sill
Watching you
May I wash your scars
Finally find out who you really are
May I please tug at your hem
May I drink of your water
May I have for a little while
The peace I see in others

See Me Fade

Sit on the rocks under the sun
Your pretty mouth was made for a gun
Exit all the words thoughts and plans
The press of the world and all its demands

The present is weighed rattles like a drum
Used to feel angry now you feel numb
You stand in the darkness call out a name
Did you ever imagine it ending this way?
See me fade, see me washed away

Breathing like a baby taken into arms
It's silent and black like a mile underwater
They gave you a mask perfect for your face
Gave you a number gave you a place

Are you there God? Tried to follow your plan
Tried to be everything you lodged in this man
I've walked a billion miles til my soul was too worn
Left with the urge to fall on my sword
See me fade, see me washed away

Plastic

Plastic cars in a plastic world
Plastic boy for a plastic girl
Plastic food for a plastic face
Plastic sign for a plastic place
We're all living in a latex age
Plastic gun for a plastic rage
We're all living in a latex age
Fix your credit and act your age

Pornography
Booze and red meat
Cars on the street
The desert and the sea

Plastic cars in a plastic world
Plastic money ready to burn
Plastic truth on a plastic screen
Plastic sheets and plastic dreams
We're all living in a latex age
Have a dream then give it away
We're all living in a latex age
Botox your face and deny your age

Pornography (etc.)

Leave the Stones to Their Bleeding

I taught myself how to sing
But all the girls like the boys with high voices now
The radio is a wasteland
All mumbles and shit falling down stairs
Sleep was such a beautiful thing
But I guess I have awoken
Not all wounds become scars
Some remain open

You can wear my boots
I'll wear your blood colored dress
We'll live a billion lives
And make each one a complete mess
You can wear my boots
I'll wear your blood colored dress
Only self-consciously conscious
In a conscious effort to be effortless

Your car smells like my past
There's a terrible song on the radio
I want to tell you to shut it off
But then you start singing along
It feels like you're flying when there's ice on the tires
Leaving a beautiful world behind
Too good for us liars

So many things I'd explain to you
If you were still breathing
So many things I'd explain to you
If my words weren't in hiding
And, oh my love it hurts
When you realize you were dreaming
Waking up with eyes in the dirt
Leave the stones to their bleeding...

Riot is a Color

A billion crows were circling
On the day we died
There was ash in the water
And no one left to cry
Closing our eyes, wishing for ghosts
Swaying slow in shiny shoes
Reflecting sequined clothes
As they sang doo doo doo doo
Doo doo doo doo (multiple times)

We left the close on the memory lines
Set a boat out and away
The water approached with angry arcs
The sky became a brooding shade of gray
Do you remember?
Will we ever find our way?
Do you remember?
Woah, yeah yeah yeah
How the ghosts were singing
Doo doo doo doo doo doo (multiple times)

You can steal a car you can take a lover
But nothing matters when it's over
Violence sets a smell in the air
And riot is a color….

Rick Ross Beard

I'm a man I can go anyplace
With the latest cell phone pubic hair on my face
Rick Ross Beard
Fuck your pups with their silicone balls
What's in my FTLs is smokin' like a Pall Mall
Rick Ross Beard

I've got diamondside seats
Discount meat
An otter named Pete--Rick Ross Beard
I'm off the chain
Singing in the rain
Knock off Rogaine--Rick Ross Beard

End of the world, time to freak
Catching the paper to a stolen beat
Rick Ross Beard
Coming up short when you're acting tall
Eyes faded like a for lease sign in a strip mall
Rick Ross Beard

I've got the bald pate
Werewolf face
Barney pants to rock the place--Rick Ross Beard
I've got International Male
Money for bail
A vestigial tail--Rick Ross Beard...

Won't Wash Today

Won't wash today, won't wash today
My fate grew running footsteps
The earth turned round
Stared too long in the mirror
Found myself below the ground
You said: "Remember those who love you,
let them find you in the dark"
It hurt too much to keep waiting
Took an extension cord to the park

Won't wash today, won't wash today
Maybe this city should burn
Write out these lost dreams with fire
Maybe we'll only be free
Whatever that means
When the dragons in us tire
Scales peel, life slinks off like a liar
Dreams hollow like imaginary superstars
Taking bored selfies in fractured yards

The paper girls and cutout boys
Waiting for some beauty
Posing through the noise
Posing like a dying woman
Waiting by the phone
To hear of her lost children
Who've had lost children of their own...

The Day Cary Grant Died

Stop being so sexy
You didn't say that, it was the alcohol
Us, too shy for sobriety
Outlands of the party, backs to the wall

I hear music every fucking day
In my head when you're talking to me
Waiting for an answer
There is no answer, fucking leave me be
I wore a suit, I took the LSD
I hid in a closet and ruled the silver screen
I was so much more beautiful than you
But now baby I'm dead

Gather the drink up devils
It's nearly two, find your shoes, last call
Look up, the moon is in trouble
Guiding us through things we won't remember at all

I hear music every fucking day
In my head when you're talking to me
Waiting for an answer
There is no answer, fucking leave me be
I wore a suit, I took the LSD
I hid in a closet and ruled the silver screen
I was so much more beautiful than you
But now baby I'm dead

Picture Perfect

Murder me, baby
Your words bring an ice age
Murder me, darling
Put a pen to the page

It's so easy, your lips look so wet
Dreams just a credit check away
Live life picture perfect
I'll bleed so lovely, give your sickness a name

Date rape eyes
Hold in the darkness
Polish those lies
Sell by the dozen

It's so easy, your lips look so wet
Dreams just a credit check away
Live life picture perfect
I'll bleed so lovely, give your sickness a name

Like a Secret Kiss

Can't you feel me breathing...
Like I'm alive in your veins?
It feels like there is no solution
And it could go any way
You mastered the language
With nothing to say
This close to breaking
And then She'll take me away

Too much skin in the evening
Too much flesh on the move
You made your skin too rough
For my unsteady hands to soothe
Sidle up like a secret kiss
Steal my breath so slowly
Sidle up like a secret kiss
As you pretend to know me...

Broken Dancer

Remember when you were light on your feet
Saying you heard the music of spring
But the world keeps making ghosts
And in crept the minor keys
You found a warm and sunny place
Crept over the weeks with some delusion of grace
But the pain was over-reaching
Taking on new shades over-achieving

The middle aged shapes
Under your youthful clothes
Closer now to the fall
The broken dancer inside you knows

Her body comes at you
In rises and runs
The smell of blood making currents
Coloring the heat bringing lions
Burn every memory
The darker hours bring the chill
Have another drink, sitting closer
The bars close you do what you will

At some point someone is going to break in your house
Rifle though all the secrets when no one is around
All these cold places we scramble for love
Pulling strangers in to hear our sounds
Picking the wrong crimes for which to atone
Sometimes we wreak things because it's all we know
Shaping faces in a desperation not to die alone
But, for some, that's how the end always goes...

Like Children

Remember when I put my heart in a bag
Set it alight at your front door
Rang the bell and ran
Watch you stomp it out from afar
Lit a cigarette with shaky hands
Thought thoughts I scarcely understand
Neighborhood windows were ajar
They probably thought me mad as I sped off in my car

Crying in your hands
The cats looking on
One moment we had each other
But now that moment is gone
These things start off bright
Like children allowed to come alive
Somethings burn forever
Some lights eventually die

Holding hands in the classroom
Bring it all the life
Say your name in a heated moment
In the place where you lie
Met your eyes in a bar
After the end of the rain
We had memories of the same places
Now memories are all that remain

Crying (etc.)

Gather

Love exists, you wild things gather
Love exists, takes shape like a last breath
Clear eyes seeing something
In a corner of a room where there's nothing
Love exists, taking ever evolving shapes
Such a violent scary thing
You can run but you'll never escape

So--you tell me
Where the light goes
So so so so so
Sown
Sewed up
Pinned trapped in
Do you remember how it begins?
Learning to walk to talk
When words and motion are unknown

Love exists, your wild things gather
Twisting in uneasy turns
As rude firelight spatters
The shadows with chaotic warmth
Learn to open your arms
Like a vein to a needle
Learn to open your arms
It's useless to fear, fear is the only evil

So--you wrote your name on my arm
If I squint I can see it
Smell your scent as you put pressure on my skin
Each time I breathe I feel it
Say every word you know to me
And I'll teach you a hundred more
The brain puts up walls calls them wisdom
The heart is a madman looking for a door…

Carry

Staring at tire fires
Imagining witches circling in the smoke
Knowing I never drew your picture
All the things your image evokes

I will cross deserts
Hug rude coastlines
Gather up the converts
Sweep through cities
Not bothering to learn names
And I will carry this love with me

Life leaves its casual wounds
Sometimes alcohol and sex soothes
Sometimes they make the scars itch
You know I would be rich
If I had a dime for every breath
I took adoring you
But adoration won't raise towns
Adoration isn't the music of animal sounds
Two people make when no one is around
I will cross deserts (etc.)

The witches rise and circle, my dear
I inhale the danger close my eyes
Feel a little sorrier
For myself, no point trying to disguise
The wind brings the smoke to me
Running over my skin like a lover
There is nothing but truth now
That everything precious is over...

The Fury

Did I put the words out there?
Say too much yet again
Just another fool perfecting messes
Waiting for every ending to begin
The fury is dying
Hear it struggling to breath
The fury is dying
Everytime you leave

Once there was madness in the air
I think you know it's name
Was not aware it hurts to be sane
After the last bright red song has been played
Did the suicide lights capture your form?
Fluttering softly, looking for someplace warm
Like a lost bird, small and afraid
A fury of wings, patterns being made

I once chased down a fury
Or maybe it pursued me
And now the fury is dying
Everytime you leave...

The Stabbing Room

She takes him to the stabbing room
An easy smile, a filmy ruse
A ruse with a view
Good enough for the desperate two
She takes him to the stabbing room
Her face is warm, he kicks off his shoes
Something will die before they're through
Trust murdered, but what can you do?

B-e-t-r-a-y
A-L

In the glow the lovers laze
He tells her of his red cap days
She speaks of emptiness and pain
Someone ignoring her again and again
The wounded making more wounds
Scars can be mistaken for tattoos
Broken glass for precious jewels
In the easy light of the stabbing room

B-e-t-r-a-y
A-L

She takes him (etc.)

Orange Thread

There's ink on your skin
The boys are coming out in droves
They've got their dicks in their hands
Nodding like you're someone they know
Words that die in your throat
Come through your hands
Moving through a broken life
No one understands

If you want to get lost
You can always follow me
I'll hide your secrets for you
Give them a burial at sea
But the waves are unpredictable
They'll fuck with your plans
Pull your hidden truth on an orange thread
Expose it on land
All those things once desirable
Locked away in shame
And I'll be the one holding your hair
When no one remembers your name...

Aground

It's a beautiful night
And there's blood in your veins
Alcohol in your blood
Just enough, oh my love
Just enough
Brace yourself
When life runs aground
Brace yourself
For the final perfect shatter
Brace yourself
Now that it's over

It's a beautiful night
The waves are perilous and warm
It's a beautiful night
For all those things for which you were warned
Just enough, oh my love
Just enough
There's a strange name
Blowing up your phone
Now you're out there somewhere
And you're probably not alone
Just enough, oh my love
Just enough

A Zone

Fog on the windows night is quiet and still
The road is empty,you'll do what you will
We get numb, go in a zone
Do it well, do it alone

Let's get fucked up
Line up to die
Eyes hard, lips not moving
Why why why why

We get numb, go in a zone
Do it well, do it alone
Now that I've seen your hands
We can both falsely atone

There's dust on the dashboard
Shaking as you roll up those bills
There's dust on the dashboard
It flickers like the eyes of those girls
I know, you lost the touch
Someone reaching out to you
I know, you lost the touch
Lost everything good in you
Come close, whiskey on your breath
Somehow I still love you
Come close, love is like an invitation to death
And I will always embrace you

GET OUT OF THE CAR

Get out of the car, up the walkway you go
He is waiting inside always inside you
I see him in your eyes when you lower yourself to kiss me
Shaky hands drawing maps of where we want to be
Casting shapes of imaginary lovers
I will watch your window for movement but not get any closer

       Always an excuse can you smell murder in the room
       Does it speak to you when you try to sleep
       Feel that splinter as it burrows deep
       My beautiful love where are you now
       Like a child breaking things looking for more
       You say you want to go home but we've gone too far
       Grab your purse, get out of the car

How your red hair came alive in the bedroom lights
How I'd smile as you'd flay me alive
Get out of the car while the light is still red
A whisper a witness a drop of blood on the bed

       Get so scared all you can do is laugh
       And the world is breathing accidents
       Smell the world on your clothes
       All the fucked up places you went
       You chose where you live my love deeper and closer to him my love
       This pulse has gone underground only beating when no one's around

Say the light will never go out, say we will never die
Alone
Say that it's someplace we'll never go
A scared heart beats faster
Anxiety collects like breath on a window
And I will carry this, carry this love wherever I go
Carry this love for you

       We will find some peace somewhere

Let it collect like cobwebs in our hair
As we walk down unknown paths
In this wild wild world
And say it again, say we'll never die alone
Say it's someplace we'll never go
And I will carry this, carry this love wherever I go
Carry this love, for you

Get
Out
Of
The
Car

Shtarker

You can run run run
Drive on through the night
But there's always someone
Who knows what hurts you and takes delight
It comes like a wasp sting
Minute and yet profound
One moment you're fully upright
The next you're on the ground

You want to burn down the house
Gouge out their eyes
Break it down to smaller and smaller pieces
Choke the memories until they die
It comes like a wasp sting
Minute and yet profound
One moment you're fully upright
The next you're on the ground

Who really is to blame?
Well, who has the blood on their hands?
The tell tale smell of copper
That a true killer understands
You can erase all the pictures
But the past still exists
You can take a million clever detours
But the shtarker knows your twists
You can erase all the pictures
But the past still exists
You can take a million clever detours
But the shtarker knows your twists…

Blindfold

Put on a blindfold to take in the view
You know
I never stop loving you
Put on a blindfold to take in the view
Oh my love
No one is coming to the rescue
This world is charring
Soon to be ash
Everything disintegrating
Going fast
And I never stop loving you
I whisper that and other pointless stuff
No matter how much I love you
It was never enough
Put on a blindfold to take in the view
You know
I never stop loving you
Some events possibly not kind
Sometimes I wonder if you've lost your mind
But you know
I never stop loving you...

Trapped in a Juice Box

The irrelevant things
We ask people who do not care
Dissolute dissolving
In the golden springtime air
Trapped in a juice box
Dropping my gold pan to stare into the distance
Trapped in a juice box
Pulled into your off kilter arhythmic dance

Oh but I love your shape
Barely hanging on seduced by the grape
Oh but I love your shape
Razors in your smile as you seal my fate

Sometimes I don't wanna hear what you call music
Singing to strangers you believe are your friends
Emotions are elements colliding in fusion
Their sparks will haunt us until the end

Oh but I love your shape (etc.)

You don't mix alcohol with wine
You don't fall for those who will leave you behind
You don't underestimate weight that can compromise your spine
And I understand you are no longer mine
You don't shed blood
It cannot be replaced
And I wish I felt nothing
Whenever I see your face

Oh but I love your shape (etc.)

30 Second Song

Why did you make me a vulnerable man?
I hear your voice, take another dram
Why did you make me a vulnerable man?
Why did you reveal who I really am?
Why did you make me a vulnerable man?
I hear your voice, take another dram
Why did you make me a vulnerable man?
Why did you reveal who I really am?

Franzia Crisp White

I'm on the Tour d' Franzia
Wheels turning going nowhere
I think I remember how to ride
Like I remember the smell of your hair

I'm exercising
Exercising my right
To see nothing
Nothing but the stars tonight
Falling out my sleeves
Higher than a kite
On the possibilities
And Franzia Crisp White

I'm drowning in a wave of nostalgia
Arms moving, oh take me towards the air
Maybe I should let myself sink
You seem smart, what do you think?
Oh what do you care
I want to tell you how beautiful
You've always been to me
But I'm scared, like everyone seems to be
Scared and on the wrong side of 40

I'm exercising (etc.)

Fuck fuck fuck it all
If it bites, makes you bleed
Fuck fuck fuck it all
That last half smile you gave me
That's all I need
And Franzia Crisp White
Franzia Crisp White
Franzia Crisp White

The Devil's Breath

When the Devil sleeps
She dreams of me
Falling into a cold stillness
Tangled in some reeds
Playing broken notes
Broken like a dying man's teeth
I could run a million miles
If I only could remember how to breathe

When the Devil sleeps
She lays down with me
Skin so cold it changes whether
Summer will ever get ahead of winter
Sometimes a brilliance comes to me
Smiles and then decides to flee
And I am haunted by this
All these possibilities
Brushing past til they're far behind me
And I could run a million miles
If I could only get to my feet
And I could run a million miles
If I could only remember how to breathe

Message Unsure

This heart is on the rocks
Beating broken bruised beyond
Tick ticking like an undersea clock
Measuring the minutes that have gone
So much time coming up with an alias
When no one was looking for you
So much time, but no one was coming near
Trial always certain message unsure

The first hit leaves you with a question
The second with a welt
The third a wound that will become a scar
What a curse these things that must be felt
You were breathing in anxiety
And exhaling doubt and uncertainty
All this undirected love I feel
Have no idea how it came to be
You were breathing in anxiety
Dragging on it like a Marlboro Light
All this undirected love I feel
I just don't have the strength to fight

Skipping Above the Knee

I'm the viceroy of vice
Sugar and spite and other paths to delight
I see you lonely
Cut open by a world that doesn't care
I see you frightened
Just a little too aware

You're perfect,a little paranoid
You close your eyes everything feels like corduroy
I see you lonely
Cut open in a world that doesn't care
I see you frightened
There, there, there, there, there

Your problem is attempting to be sane
In a world that is deranged
Trying to plant your feet on solid ground
In the middle of sea
In 2020 we've banished safety
Sanity, security
Pick the leaves off the vine
Chop a line drink the wine
You'll feel better when you feel nothing
Often nothing is better than something

I see you lonely
Cut open by a world that doesn't care
I see you frightened
There, there, there, there,there....

What Was it All Worth?

They say that star you landed on
Was the loneliest place on the universe
Silly spaceman
What was it all worth?
La la la la la la la la
What was it all worth?
Through the atmosphere
Beyond all your hopes and fears
What was it all worth?
La la la la la la la la

We write our future
With our aspirations
And one day it all ends
And there's no negotiation
What was it all worth?
La la la la la la la la
What was it all worth?
Little low man
Shooting so high
No one even pausing
When you prepare to say goodbye
What was it all worth?
La la la la la la la la
What was it all worth?

The moon is in misfortune
Some people can't afford to breath
Do you know why people don't look back
Whenever they leave?
What was it all worth?
La la la la la la la la
What was it all worth?
La la la la la la la la….

Free To Be Free

A smudge to clear the air
A smudge to blur the words
A smudge like the smell of autumn
Leaves burning
Take the wrong drug the wrong lover
Always falling
Waiting for peace, waiting for a touch
Waiting for solace, and the pain of waiting leads to malice

       Take a little space
       You put a lot of space out there
       Take a little space
       Something sharp in the air
       You cannot kill the dead
       You can only build their armies in your head
       Waiting for peace (etc.)

You can smash it all to fragments
Pieces sharp like memories
You are what you're gonna be
Because you're free to be free
I see that spark of freedom of you, see you turn it ugly
--A knife finds your hand, your hand finds my back
You've got a bag full of plans
But so does the Devil
You're a model for these times, of greed deception and weakness
An avatar of avarice, so, explain why I still feel love for you

It's nothing--it's just idiots doing what idiots do
It's nothing--saying that doesn't make it true

Waiting for peace (etc.)

> You can smash it all to fragments
> Pieces sharp like memories
> You are what you're gonna be, because you're free to be free
> I see that spark of freedom of you, see you turn it ugly
> It's an age of taking heroes, and shooting them against a wall
> It's how you package your heartlessness
> It's just a shame that's all

Waiting for peace (etc.)

Free To Be Free

The Devil Is Blowing You a Kiss

You have this offhand sensual burn
And the smoke is making me dizzy
I wrote your name on a card
Whispered it in the dark as if I could conjure you
Yeah, all these things you need
Maybe none of them are me
But there's magic out there for you
Just close your eyes and breathe

Leave the thirsty man fumbling for the dice
After the last river has run dry
Broken skin lips blood and dust
Threw out my back rolling my eyes
Playing off this ache you left in me
Don't try and tidy up this beautiful mess
Nearly broke my neck
Watching you walk away in that dress

Open your eyes
The Devil is blowing you a kiss
Offering you smoke
Promising you fire
And you bow to his words
Laugh at every barbed joke
Unable to admit you were wrong
Even as you weep and choke

Bowie's Ghost

I'll be out there
Breeding a little resistance with Clan McGregor
The light turns yellow you laugh with some friends
Who aren't actually there

Bowie's ghost is at the window
You smell his cigarette before you see him
Oh baby, did you ever know to run?
You laugh too easy sitting on your feet
Suck down the dregs
It's nearly midnight and there are people to meet

Goddamn this world is fucked
And you're a sweet thing dying to be held
Embraces breed complications
And you don't have reservations
It's four, the cigarettes are gone
There are shapes out there in the dark
Coming out of nowhere like the first notes of a song...

Running

I crossed the mountains, I crossed the rivers
I crossed the deserts, I never stopped running
Days flowed like wine
I got ahead, fell behind
But I never stopped running

Worlds erupted from the dirt
Built up, glowed, and then fell away
I had so many words, no idea what to say
But I never stopped running
I saw the beauty of the world, saw the pain
I had to close my eyes--
Then open them again
And I never stopped running

You and I have no idea why we're here
Why a minute is a minute and a year a year
You and I thought we knew why we're here
But one day you wake up
And there's another face in the mirror
We're all just actors
Throwing makeup on all this defeat
You draw another breath
Step out of the light to find your feet
And keep running…

Boppin' to the KTEL

It's all KTEL's *Sorry I Gave You VD* classics up in here
Cheap whiskey, the smell of cedar and beards
Spray a little Lysol on that shit it'll be okay
Put on the mall walking shoes rub on the Ben Gay
Time to get on up and then get on down
Scratchin' like you got the crabs
Three term mayor of Sexytown

It's all KTEL's *Sorry I Gave You VD* Classics up in here
Cocaine, easy smiles, rollerskates, feathered hair
A little Seals and Croft, Chicago, and Jefferson Air
Shake out the polyester, purring like a Dustbuster
Umbrella drinks, propositions, another line
Waterbed positions
Grinning like a politician
There's a line up at the bar but I'll win this election

It's all KTEL's *Sorry I Gave You VD* Classics up in here
Chest hair chains and misogyny lines
Melting all over you like a vinyl seat red vine
It's three past one and my zipper is half down
And your the most beautiful person now that
no one else is around...

The Unicorn Song

Breath real hard
There's a man in the dark
Laying out charges
You know you're on the list
Falling over like a drunken ship
No one told you life would hurt like this
Bite your tongue and make a fist
You're going to have to
Fight your way out of this abyss
Even if it feels so good to sink
Kick your shoes off, have another drink

There's a broken glass love
Cutting like a criminal through a crowd
The present is a series of thoughts
You dare not say out loud
Maybe you should have asked for help
But it's always too late when you're proud
No one told you life would hurt like this
Bite your tongue and make a fist
You're going to have to
Fight your way out of this abyss
Own some of the blame
Because it's one of the few things in this world
You can rightfully claim
We all die in single bulb rooms
Feeling the color slowly drain
We all die in single bulb rooms
Hoping someone we love will remember our name...

The Patron
Saint of
Nothing and Nowhere

The future is a breath you keep holding
Until the lack of oxygen in your lungs
Hopefully makes the visions come
Can someone so certain feel unsure?
Bobbing in the current like a colorful lure
And the allure of being lost has a cost
Accosted by the cliches that attracted you the most

I made a pact with my weaknesses
To sleep until we're through this
But they betrayed me when I closed my eyes
Came roaring to life like a 442 in the drive
The sex of spent fuel moving up the exhaust
Exhausted, no one ever teaches you the cost
Of feeling shit because feelings expand in the air
Like the mattress you sleep on alone when they are no longer there
Did you really sleep? Did anyone think that lie was true?
Did you really sleep? Now who is fooling whom?

The pressure when your heroes become your peers
When the game is lost but everyone wants to cheer
Kneeling to the patron saint of nothing and nowhere
Caught like a careless bee in her rust colored hair
Every calculating twist like a raven in the wind
Watching for something good, working towards a happier end
Every calculating twist like a raven in the wind
Tearing at the fabric you should really try and mend...

Whiskey Rules

There's a gulf between us
And I find myself swimming in the icy dark
Do you ever see the bubbles?
No, I don't think you do
Coaxing flames, spreading rumors
Grief is a funny thing when you've got a sick sense of humor

Measuring empty space
In all these green bottles
Lined up like judges
Almost holy in the sunlight
I've got a congregation of holy fools
Walking haunted roads
Past the last school
And I don't want to be taught anymore
Slinking off lawless
Only governed by whiskey rules

Burning through
Like a fast paced tune
One I tried to sing to you
My voice was strong
My heart was true
But it wasn't enough
And there was nothing I could do
Burning through
Both ends turning to ash then falling
All these words are meaningless
Cause now it's another language you're speaking
All these words are meaningless
Dead matches next to trash cans...

Righteous You Fell

I chased you all up and down these walls
Until my legs and heart meant nothing at all
Joining your collection of bathwater babies
Left on the side of the road as you were escaping
Your shape put words in my mouth
I knew not to spit out
Your shape put together a bunch of words
Nearly all better not heard

Saw you knocking on God's back door
Don't you see She doesn't believe in you anymore
Didn't you see?
Maybe it wasn't God, maybe it was just me
All these burdens we are unaware even exist
Until they're on our backs or in our arms
All these burdens going from buzz to swarm
Sometimes I wonder if your blood is even warm

It's such a tricky thing
A non religious man sorting out his faith
Sitting up at one am wide awake
Categorizing all those open wounds
Putting them under lights for the bored to view
It's such a tricky thing
That lust that finds us when we're all alone
Every heartbeat swallowed by the silence
You paint on the walls in a desperation to atone
For the failures of the one who finds you in the mirror
Is it a sin of the flesh that you fear?
That uneasy ache from the hard truth you find
That cheap glass isn't telling any lies
Righteous you fell, only black cards played
Your faith should have been a reed and not a stone
Turning away those who would leave flowers on your grave
When you die unbent but alone...

Temptation

Was this the life you drew on a napkin?
Before the sky grew heavy and wet
Turned the streets into mirrors
Turned your plans into a Rorschach test
It was better laid plans
That got you in this mess
Often better laid plans
Are best undressed

Your skin sent a message
But I was in the other room
Your skin sent a message
But I was in the other room
Lying on a broken bed
Like a pharoah in his tomb

Luxurious strangers
Are falling off your roof
This is the age of consent
But there isn't any proof
Sometimes
You really should build a jail for your words
Sometimes
The deaf just want to be heard

I'm going to toss out the oars
Give myself to the stuttering waves
I'm going to toss out the oars
Give myself to the stuttering waves
You know, sometimes I'm tempted
To give the Devil a raise
You know sometimes I'm tempted
But what is temptation doing for me these days?

Another Car

We are grace with stress cracks
The bars are all closed and there's water on the tracks
That give your skin an insinuation
Of lost days with no inhibitions

How many nows did you surrender to yesterday
Tried to feel, trying to fuck the pain away
Hope and fears collide make patterns inside
You just jumped in another car, hoping to ride
It's just suburbs, no stations coming in
Jumping out of your skin, your clothes, falling into him

We are grace with stress cracks
The bars are all closed and there's water on the tracks
Touch your arm realize everyone is looking
Didn't you want them to ask why you're falling?
There's millions of murders on paper
You're tightly wound like a soldier
Do you remember when you didn't depend on your blood
To align all these twisted stars
Do you remember when it was easy to love?
Before you climbed in another car
Do you remember
I think I recall your memory being better than most
Do you remember
When I was more to you than a ghost?

The *Witch*

Run down by desperate cars on limitless streets
Lost in the rhythm of your steps
Where only fools and lovers meet
I'm the random thought moving down your neck
I'm circling you like every desperate breath
Watching, watching
Drifting
Only the faded chip walls
Witness your pacing
Only the faded chip walls
And the spirit of what I used to be

A lie
Alive
The world is barbed like a cruel aside
Take another breath
Just don't ask me why
All the things pulling you
Pulling you to pieces
Sometimes I wish I was truly evil
Casting spells and circling omens
Sometimes I wish I was truly evil
Get in your head and burst it open

I've read the ashes
I've studied the sky for portents
You're building a house with your new man
Building up to disappointment
I've seen beauty and grace in you
Precious things inside I saw spark and glint
I've seen beauty and grace in you
Precious things inside I saw spark and glint
I've seen beauty and grace in you
I just wonder where the hell it went

This Universe

The honey tricks have been laid
The predators are writing checks
The honey tricks have been laid
The predators are writing checks
Rally round the fallacy, boys
The shits nearly up to your necks
Figure out what you see in me
Cause you're seconds from my net

If you leave me in this universe
I'll take a break and through a fit
If you leave me in this universe
I'm bound to become the center of it
There are numbers on paper
And borrowed minutes like soldiers you chose to kill
This universe would keep spinning
If only I'd stand still

Why are you so angry?
I thought you loved that road you're running down
It would easy to be angry
When something beautiful is laid in the ground
Why are you so angry?
Don't you know there's transcendence in pain?
Your dark moods have their own weather
And I'm soaked to the skin again

Regents

Everything is flowering
There's the scent of blood in the air
Animals driven by piston thoughts
As they writhe in their lairs
Claws making rhythms on the pavement
Rigid in shape and intention
As you rollerskate with that smile in your face
I sense is mostly invention
       What do you see now--
       Looking through your smoked glass?
       Do you see them crawling to you--
       Through this world of hard ons and masks?
       See the indecisive shape shifter
       Taking his cigarette break
       The smoke pulls you into your memories
       But half of them are fake
The regents are in atrophy
Cause there are only ruins to rule
Someone stole all the words
Before burning down the school
The regents curse
Their teleprompters and their flunkies
Cause there's no more stones hinting blood
And it's fashionable to be unlucky
       Everything is flowering
       Did you hope that'd include you?
       Handed all the time in the world
       With not a thing to do
       You thought all your problems would end
       When you found someone for the throne
       You dreamed of bottomless love and desire
       When you found someone for the throne
       But all this pain is for nothing
       Because we all die alone

Coagulant

It's not blood, you see
Just yesterday's news out on the table
Heat comes out
Of where it was offered
Wrapping around you
Like a rosewood coffin
You know I love you
My senses can't follow what my brain learned
You know I love you
But I'm ready to let it all burn

The Word took you places
I doubt you could find on a map
The Word showed you love
Lured you into a trap
It's not blood you see
What holds it all together
Is hardly a mystery
Just the most foolish part of me
You know I will always have love for you
Forget? Like I ever knew how
You know I will always have love for you
But everything's different now...

If Ever I Should Cross Your Mind

Do you remember the way?
Between your house and mine?
There was a lightness to the late Spring air
Hours of cigarettes and wine
Both of us losing track of time
When this sort of thing has its hooks in you
Real life becomes a pantomime
Those days are lost to us
Moments among the best of us
If ever I should cross your mind
Not sure when, not sure how
If ever I should cross your mind
It's too late now

I remember walking these streets
When they led to where you slept
Everything between us drifted down from the ceiling
And settled on the boards until they were swept
When I see what you've done
Disagreeing parts of me go to war
When I see what you've done
Trapped in this mess like feathers in tar
When I see what you've done
I'm not sure who you are
Those days are lost to us
Moments among the best of us
If ever I should cross your mind
Not sure when, not sure how
If ever I should cross your mind
It's too late now...

My True Face Waits

A plague came to town making everything meaningless
Lazy flakes of snow falling
On your simple summer dress
And the ghosts in shirtsleeves
Won't let you surrender the past
Stole your shoes while you slept
Paved the world with broken glass

You said those designed to receive love
Are lost to give it
So shine a light on what I feel and I will refute it
You said it's only the selfish
Who truly understand themselves
So why do I feel like a pauper--
When you accuse me of great wealth?

Isn't that the way it always is?
You take a long breath and make a wish--
I wish our life together hadn't been a speeding car
Destin to be driven into a ditch
Does it feel like we're reaching
Higher out of hell
Only to be pulled back down
By our lower selves

You chose to sail around the planet
When the earth became flat
Shoved some diamonds in your pocket
And said that's that
Maybe all the windows are barred
But the key is under the mat
Believe me this deception
Is for the best as the mask falls into place
So forgive me when I lead you to believe
This mask isn't my true face

The Year When No One Could Breathe

Fruit on the stem
Changes on the whim
An owl in the eye
Of a wind like a whirlpool
No words kill the tracker
The ice man in your footsteps
Seconds from his hands around your neck
Seconds
And now those seconds have passed--
Fruit on the stem, once ripe now rotten
So sweet we fall to decay
Details to get caught in
Once I bore down for you
Swallowed words I needed to spit
It might have been the wrong thing
But you know I'd do it again
No words kill the spectre
Growing limbs in this nightmare
The dream of every breath
From this moment to the next--
I was the middle of a fever
The night you didn't come home
Sleeping in a distant motel
Knew even then you weren't alone
I stab this hurt in the eye in the guts, in the throat
But it won't fucking die
There's no map to get out of here
And the cliffs are closing in
The water quickly rising
The panic setting in--
Fruit on the stem
Hanging, but gravity is ticking
Cool calm determined
Fruit on the stem hanging,desperate
But gravity is wise and ever determined

The Howling

I get angry with myself
For letting the wild things in
Oh, I knew they were out for blood
Heard it in their fevered din
Heard it in their howling
Should have kept the door barred
Embrace the solitude that had found me
Ignore the thrashing in the yard---
I get angry with myself
Even if you say I'm not entirely to blame
I saw the wild things curled up on the porch
Looking so tame
But if I had decided to be wise
Taken a closer stare
I would have seen the murder in their eyes
That I didn't have a prayer---
Oh, they ripped out my throat
And stole into the night
Fluttered off like a ribbon in the breeze
Left just a withered husk of me---
I'm losing it
Can't make sense at all
If you see my shit
Kindly give me a call----
I drink like a fish
Scarred from the hook
Since the wild things gathered
To drink their fill at my brook---
May I thought I could howl myself
Run with the best of them
But they dropped off like a stone in a well
Just split like an atom
Maybe I thought I could howl myself
Grow fur and teeth and venom
But the wild things are not easily sated
And maybe I'm a bit too domesticated

History

Be it the guru on the mountain
Or the scared man in a cave
We're all trying to find a little love
Before the embrace of the grave
Whether soaring like a bird
Or twisting like a serpent in the sun
There are things they keep us rooted
And things that make us run

I stumbled into seven years
Lost in a darkened saloon
I knew you in the unforgiving sun
And in the shade of a contemplative moon
I will travel far
Where the dirt is dry and the trees wet
No matter how many years fall before me
I'll remember exactly how we met
No matter how many years fall before me
You're someone I will never forget

Be it the guru on the mountain
Or the scared man in a cave
We're all trying to find a little love
Before the embrace of the grave
The end is rarely easy
Regret, fear, slashes of black and red
The end is rarely easy
Few go calm on their deathbed
The end is rarely easy
You could say the same for you and me
But whether we can admit it or not
We're a part of each other's history
Agony and triumph, love and misery
We'll always be a part
Of each other's history...

Everything's Fine

The quiet girl in the murderous Ford
Don't go that way if you're unsure
The quiet girl in the murderous Ford
Lost in the trees a week in the world
The lights come up, you've been out late
The click of insect addicts
Night air like water, you're throwing out bait

No one gets inside now
Secrets like spiderwebs crossing half lit rooms
No one gets inside now
The graffiti says something's wrong with you
Marks on the walls like a Rorschach test
She's a million miles away now
In your mind always getting undressed

The traffic builds
Everything hidden starts to tighten
Your breath a shaky line
Waiting for a voice to say everything's fine

The wind dies, the banners grow lazy
Words break up, thoughts you meant to share
Look around, is this where you want to be?
Words break up, cannot be repaired
Words break up
Impatient, she starts to stare
Words break up
Coming out in fragments, dissolving in the air...

VG

I will always remember the day
That I was okay with you not loving me anymore
I think of Van Gogh
Shooting himself in a field
A wound that wouldn't heal
All the colors he revealed
That you or I could never see
What was he thinking?
Out there in the lazy wheat?
A poor man's shoes on his feet
He made us see the sunflowers
And the starry starry night
But he couldn't see another day
The crows circled to carry him away

I will always remember the day
That I was okay with you not loving me anymore
I've got a bunch of paintings
Locked away in the basement
Look at them less and less
As the months pick up the weeks days and moments
Two people in love
A story everyone knows
I may not go in that room for months at a time
But I will always carry the key with me
And Van Gogh shot himself in a field
And I am not a painter
I never had a grasp of such things
I misplace that key from time to time
I just know it's on a silver ring

I will always remember the day
That I was okay with you not loving me anymore
It was beautiful, I was somewhere wild

And for the first time in a long while
I could look at the world with the eyes of a child
With a dagger in his hand
What was Van Gogh thinking?
When he took his last stand
I have seen love to be beautiful
Yes, I even saw that between you and I
What was Van Gogh thinking---
After the shot, when he started to die?
Paint under his fingernails
The color of fury dripping over his belt
And there have been many times
I have cursed all the things I have felt
But I am not a painter
And I do not own a gun
And I will not stand in a field
For anyone

I remember when I was barefoot
And you bought me shoes
I remember when you showed me a crazy city
The beautiful frenzy and the views
I heard the tearing paper
When you ripped up the past and walked away
I picked up the pieces and threw them in a room
I may just walk back in someday
With a torch and some glue
But I am not a painter
And I do not own a gun
And I will not stand in a field
For anyone…

vg

Don't Send Me No Weather

I spent weeks searching the night sky
Looking for your face in the stars
But don't bother to drive by
Now I spend my time inside
The dead send their invitations
The living excuses and procrastinations
I'm a ghost who doesn't want to be real
Taking shape in a senseless world
Like a man holding a hammer
With nothing to build
      You make your choices
      And then your choices make you
      Tell me, does it rain where you are?
      Probably not like up here
      They tell you to keep your mouth closed
      While putting your shoes on
      They tell you ghosts don't know they're ghosts
      After they're gone
There are no good people
There are no bad people
Just angels and demons
Fighting over real estate
I know enough roads to wander the rest of my life
And wonder if I'll forget you by the time I die
      Do me a favor
      If you ever feel the wind picking up
      Don't send me no weather
      I know you could collect it in a box if you wanted
      But I'm too old for chasing storms
      And too tired of being haunted
      The world is a mix
      Of fury, fear, and indifference
      And regret drifting like a phantom
      Caught up like paper on a fence

The Year of Falling Apart

I left the city
Before the streets were colored red
I said goodbye to the places that we knew
I got in my car and fled
Drawing pictures of an ideal world
Until there was no ink in the pot
Looking for a place where I didn't see your face
I went to where all the maps forgot

Do you recall when we fell apart so beautifully?
I locked that picture below my room
There is always that moment of deep, profound peace
The moment before you meet your doom
I feel the fear coming off you
Rolling in slowly sparking waves
But this world was meant to be shattered
Crushed and then swept away
This world was built on broken hearts
It was nothing for us to save

Even ruins are bathed in sunlight on occasion
Causing all the ghosts to flee
If you ever sense a ghost moving through the ruins of this world
Chances are that it's me
Lovers cut themselves with broken promises
As they die they tend to glow
Marking doors at the end of the world
Signs only you and I will know

Should I
Fall Down Your Stairs

Should I fall down your stairs---
I will blame it on the gin and tonic
Spirits come solid in the dark
Not the phantoms seizing my heart
Tell me of the tall ships crossing your mind
All the hopes and dreams you left behind
Oh, the curse of hope that comes in pairs
Please forgive me when I fall down your stairs
They gave me a name forgot to write it down
They gave me a name I didn't think to write it down
You remember the love and grace we knew?
You remember the love and grace we knew?
The problem is in the end I am I and you are you
It's so simple even the fool…
Saw the end coming
Oh, you could see the sandwich board on his face
Life is hope and beauty and love and loss
All us frightened strangers looking for our place

Forgive me I fall down your stairs
My heart is in a vault somewhere
I tried to give you the key
But it died, the easy part of me
That someone who smiles at strangers
Who can welcome those he doesn't known
The one who can always be there
The one not just rattling chains like a ghost
Believe me, I'll always be living just outside your door
Wishing I knew how to pick locks and give you a little more

God, in Her wisdom, gives us a spark
God, in Her wisdom, give us a little spark
To give us strength, the hope to find the way

The courage to walk through the dark
If you see me struggling to speak
Please understand I've been pared down to the core
Once I was young, the door opened to anyone
Now it's locked forevermore...

should i fall down your stairs

The Raven

You've got a mountain of mistakes to fall down
Clowns in the pipeline
You're in the clothes of another man
And out of your mind
Holding onto the belief
That the world is your joke
As the fires ice over
And the oceans start to smoke

The sunrise birds are singing
But in a key you do not know
Blindfolded, mapping disasters
Sleeping where the vines of suspicion grow
The priest has dirt under his nails
And a smile like a haunted door
Your beautiful bed shimmers like a curse
The wise men sleep on the floor

The banners of the fool snap
In a vain and dirty breeze
You can wait and bait your traps
You are free to do as you please
You can sweep it all your way
But in the end we're bound to lose everything
You can have it all
But you're just walking in your sleep
And when your eyes finally open
Chances are, I won't be there
I was the raven outside your window
Now I am far off in the air

The   Cable

You lied to me as a fever burned
When the truth came it was in code
Broken words coming over underwater cables
Metal cables, they tend to corrode
Language gets twisted
Those off the shoulder things you said to me
Even smoothed out it was just gibberish
What didn't you just say what you mean?

> Someone's rolling the bones
> In a by the hour hotel room
> You don't see the threes and fours
> You are like a dying man watching a door
> Will love ever come walking through?
> Why can't I fly like I do in dreams?
> I never really knew, how to talk to you
> Why didn't you just say what you mean?

Our love is dead, you said
A plane ticket in your clenched hand
Some planes soar through clouds
Some planes crash before they land
I'm on a different sort of plane
Just drifting like a kite in the breeze
I used to let you hold the string
Why didn't you just say what you mean?

> We can deny it
> But there's always a cable stretched from you to me
> Love never truly dies, it just changes
> Love can be graceless, causing derangements
> Beauty and ugliness, demons and angels

> We're just leaves floating down a lonely stream

Sometimes drifting apart, sometimes colliding
Now there is only to wonder
What you and I could have been
If I had ever answered you
Why didn't you just say what you mean?

the cable

Funkee Toof Luv

We are perfectly imperfect
Broken in all the right places
Yellowed, narrowed, and faded
People gather round
Laugh at our flaws
At our failings
It isn't galling
They just don't get our funky tooth love

I've got gaps
You've got gaps
We're pale and assailed
In a world of perma tans and caps
People lean out of their SUVs
With a snide comment for you and me
At our failings
But we're prevailing
With this, our funky tooth love

You've got bad skin and glasses
I'm the sort of guy
Only the blind and drunk would make passes
We look like the world beat us down
And they let us know
All over this stupid, shallow town
But we've doing fine
Even if our smiles are terribly misaligned
Each night you and I
Thank the stars above
For our malformed, stick armed
Funky tooth love...

The Swimming Hole/Groovy Apple

I clambered over rocks,like a much younger fool

To take in the pale green depths

Where the lazy river pooled

The water deep beguiling alive

Like every smile I've seen on your face

I imagined diving in with you

Naked, shock bumps on our skin

The sun a sighing witness, backing over the mountain

Temptation, go deeper

Temptation, go deeper

Temptation, go deeper

Take a bite, fall off the edge of the earth

And afterwards, sitting by a fire

Dark bringing its shapes

Daring the visions to come, you and I

Temptation, go deeper

Temptation, go deeper

Temptation, go deeper

Take a bite, fall off the edge of the earth

My life is like breathing underwater; I can be strong but still I falter

Thinking of you and I laying in the dark counting the stars

You can only see when you're lost

Temptation go deeper

Temptation, go deeper

Temptation, go deeper

Take a bite, fall off the edge of the earth

Do you ever think my name--when your breath comes short?

When you finally meet your maker---will you ask Her to spare a little thread?

I'll hide the matches after the house burns down

I get a strange sideways fever, whenever you're around

We're all just restless sleepers, waiting on a dream

Your name is like pollen in the air

And I circle like a bee

Your name is like pollen in the air

And I circle like a bee

the swimming hole/groovy apple

Everyone #4

The trees where the strange fruit grew
Moan when the weather comes
They've been painted red, white, and blue
Clouds overhead tight as a drum
Everyone knows everything is out of order
Everyone senses the ceiling is floor
Everyone is happy to play the contrarian
And the dogs don't know who to bite anymore

The trees where the strange fruit grew
They're ablaze with blossoms again
Alibis in the air smell like chainsaw oil
Something like poison in the wind
The bored henchmen stare at the exit sign
We're all gamblers insisting we're on a roll
Even the beautiful feel loneliness
Even Piccaso stole

The trees where the strange fruit is in bloom
Some people like to picnic in the shade
They watch the people marching in the sun
Drinks are poured and judgments made
Everyone's gotta serve somebody
Someone lost the map to this maze
Somebody better chew threw the walls
Before we kill each other in this place...

Cigarette Days

Some weeks grind you into cement
Some weeks, the pleasure comes easy
Smoke circling your unsteady friends
Before drinks and laughter come to an end
I'll see you outside
In a year, maybe more than one
You and I are locked out of the car
Taste the air; it's like sucking on a gun
You are I are locked out of the car
And you can't breathe enough to run

Who taught the sun that color?
Who trained the sky to see revenge
You're out of focus, taking a selfie
Loitering with your soft focus friends
Forgetting how to drink enough
As the cigarette days steal the hours
See you write in crayon all your claims to power
See you wilting like a flawed idea or a flower

Keep that face pinned in the closet
You should know there's no use for it
Every pretty mask coated with ash
You're a can of kerosene searching for a match
It's a world of sparks outside
Fear throws all the music in the key of melee
It's a world of sparks outside
Where dreams and fears circle and collide
It's a world of sparks outside
See them so confused, rattling the barricades
It's easier to play the mute
When all you can talk about are the mistakes you made

The Undermen

Put me in a trance, Oh, I am the Devil (3X)
Will you believe in me---when I scorch your skin? (2X)
I am the one you blame when the logic ends
I am the one you blame when it's easier to bend
Another drink, this one half spilled
Another drink, this one half spilled
How did the music in your head get so shrill?

      You put me in a trance, Oh, you are the Devil (3X)
      Will I still believe in you---when only your footprints remain? (2X)
      You're the one I blame when I walk out into the night
      You're the one I blame when it's too hard to do what's right
      Another drink, oh, sink me
      Drown me in your demons
      Another drink, oh, sink me
      I need to have worse taste in friends

You, you complain about a fear of the night
You, you complain about a fear of the night
In my head I'm wringing my hands
Why don't you turn on the fucking light?
Lou's ghost is singing *Sweet Jane* in the kitchen
Little Tom is scuffling in the closet
You claim I'm toying with the dark, with devils
But this boredom was a torment
Davy said he was afraid of Americans
I don't blame him, they talk too loud
It's funny how those with the most fear, tend to act so proud
Someday I'll side with love and light, but this is not that time
I've been on my knees looking for a compass
Since you cast me out I've been out of my mind
I've been on my knees, looking for a compass
Since you cast me out I've been out of my mind...

Portland, Burning

You told me to go back
But I am staying gone
In the pavement only seeing cracks
Every hello feels like an attack
I had to get away
Or throw myself in the river
I had to get away
But then the city grew nearer
      I had to stand by
      When they knocked off your crown
      I had to stand by
      As they burned you to the ground
      I could feel your death in my lungs
      Ten thousand bicycles crashing
      They say bravery is wasted on the young
      And Portland is burning
You told me to go back
But I'm nine days down the road
In the pavement only seeing cracks
Every hello feels like an attack
What is going through your mind---
This lonely life you choose
What is going through your mind---
To think I could just stop loving you?
      I had to stand by
      When they knocked off your crown
      I had to stand by, as they burned you to the ground
      I could taste that you were dead
      As another morning found me
      Your sweet fragile voice in my head
      All these ideas you put out in my hand
      Just things you misread
      I'll be your true awakening, if you let me go back to bed
      I had to stand by, you know, I had to let it all die…

Sideways Emperor

This life it burns then settles
This life it bursts then sighs
The ghosts close up like twilight flowers
Then open before your eyes

In ruffles and dirty velvet
The sideways emperor rolls on his heels
Nervously touching his stained cravat
The sideways emperor rolling off his heels
The executions have become boring
And there's nothing left to steal
You are cursed by what you run from
And damned by what you feel
This life it burns then settles (etc.)

Do you remember---
How you crossed the room to tell me your name?
Did you pick up on how I was struck by you?
No? Well, I made a point to look away
They're finding people frozen in ice
Hundreds maybe thousands of years old
Back then we lit a fire under each other
Ah, those days it was easier to be bold
This life it burns then settles (etc.)

Of courts and cities rising from nothing
Only to become abandoned and decay
Full of ideas and endless words
Until there's nothing left to say
This life it burns then settles
This life it bursts then sighs
The ghosts close up like twilight flowers
Then open before your eyes

White Lightning/Yard Sale Heart

These mornings come at you
Who dare tells when the seasons change
And this little monkey
Needs to invent a new monkey brain
The buildings get higher
So I stay in the wilderness
The buildings get higher
Better spit out what you can't digest

Oh my love you found a better way
Does it burn like white lightning?
Oh my love you found a different way
Did it leave you pleading to the sky for a little rain?

It'll be okay it's only money
They sit and calmly smile
Right now I'm watching you decorate
But I'll be gone in a while---
Now don't you fret
I've always got too much love for you
Now don't you fret
Over the pictures of things you cannot forget
Or over your yard sale heart
Left on a blanket on the ground
Your beautiful beautiful yard sale heart
You kept marking it down
You kept marking it down...

Chiffarobe

Some would say drinking
Is like looking through God's eyes
Some would say drinking
Is just the Devil in disguise
I would have said
It's like hearing the language of love
Even if it sings
With a twisted burning tongue

There ain't no rain in the mountains
There isn't water in the well
I ain't busting up a chiffarobe for you
I know the stories that you tell

The world is full of bathwater babies
See them reach out so scared
Sometimes you see a face on the moon
Sometimes you feel angels in your hair
You said things would change
Well, they went from bad to worse
The hours sauntered by my throat grew dry
Lord, save me from this thirst
There ain't no rain in the mountains (etc.)

Your in town jackets and out of town guests
Gather with gimlets and leave you mentally undressed
You turn a corner, you turn like milk
You turn from all the beauty in the world
And say that burlap feels like silk
There ain't no rain in the mountains (etc.)

I Was Never Really Here

Oh sweetheart, throw your darts
They will always fly clear
I am just an omen in your heart
A portent longing to stir
Your blood to a furious boil
If only I could do that with words

I was never really here
Oh, your fools may say otherwise
But I have a stone that speaks of you
And I'll keep it in my room
Until my beautiful but lonely demise

The spurned tell tales
Of new loves, re-flourishing wells
But all the dead flowers tell the truth
Just accept this from me to you

I was never really here
Paint me as a demon or a saint
A man groveling for alms in the mud
Or a raconteur in the parlors where fine ladies faint
You can paint me as an enemy
You can paint me as a friend
But I am just words dissolving in a whisper
I am just a leaf in the wind...

ROMANS

See the Romans where they fell
See their pride in repose so pale
So frail, some say the body is a jail
But maybe they'd rather be gripping bars
Staring out in anger
But anger is what got them this far
Many times this world has witnessed the potential of a man's temper

      I will agree to say your name
      But I will not go to war
      And my voice may sound different
      A little tired, a little worn
      See the Romans laughing
      As they ran across a plain
      Before the spears began to fly
      When life was just a game

You said that I did not know you
Many times, your eyes full of pain
But I saw you from the beginning
And we both knew how this would end

      See the Romans as they realize
      They have only moments that remain
      Everything replayed as they stumble
      Lovers traitors saviors sunshine and rain
      See the Romans as they realize
      They have only moments that remain
      Everything replayed as they stumble
      Lovers traitors saviors sunshine and rain

RAISED TRUCK BLUES

Amerika, toilet of the free
Get pumped Twitter drunk cargo short bro to the extreme
Mall music squires with contraband dreams
Smiling on the outside, inside feeling scared and unseen
Don't be such a pussy, you know only losers lose
Failure is unamerican, be strong and sing the raised truck blues

Pedal to the medal, speed metal time lapse
Eyes so bright inside as cold as a death mask
Go squad energy drinks in chain
Get to the gym and buy some fucking Rogaine
Rage of the Costco cowboys
Checking out the selfie girls in the Starbucks line
Driving like a video game cause I kept hittin' snooze
YouTube butt lube sing the raised truck blues

Roll your overly elegant words on home
Pure beef injection taking pictures of bones
Full throttle racing away from erectile dysfunction
Fake news, candy crew, viral video of my bunions
Chapter and verse, my country right or wrong
Whiten your teeth you socialist thief
Please don't do porn unless you've got a big dong
Ain't got a Che beard or organic hemp shoes
I've got Easy Cheese, heart disease, and the raised truck blues...

THE PINES

Drinking sentimental moonshine
Courting the smoky heirs
As they drift through the pines
Playing boom bust hopscotch
Just another lonely soul
On the sheriff's watch

I used to kiss one of the faces, that you wore
You'd check it two or three times
Before walking out the door
I would never call you baby
You're too tough for that
Remember the days of love and promise
That the wind carried away like a foolish hat

Drinking sentimental moonshine (etc.)

Home used to be one of the places, that we shared
Now the locks have been been changed
A sense of rootlessness in the air
There goes the doorbell
A man falls out the window
Grabs a beast by the tail
And pulls the day into night

Drinking sentimental moonshine (etc.)

The Parcel

Elvis sleeps at Graceland
They made a big deal of his grave
People come from far off to stare at it
And then they drive away
There's ghosts in the trenches
They don't know the war's been lost
Shimmering with expectant eyes
Scared even though they've already died
A chaotic car rushing past
Brings me back to this time and place
And a collection of memories
Violently slapping me in the face

      My parents went to college
      They worked in an industry and saved
      My parents went to college
      I slept in and dug my own grave
      And you, you left a parcel on my front step
      Before running off somewhere
      I just looked at that box
      Stupidly remembering the smell of your hair
      I just looked at that fucking box
      And of nothing else was I aware

You left a parcel on my front porch,I could not bring it inside
The rain stole its shape the sun left it scorched
And the days, I still keep score
Everyone tells me to close the blinds

But I'd still know it's there
I called the cops to report a bomb
But they were cheating at Scrabble and didn't care
Everyone tells me to close the blinds
Aunt Suzy calls in the dead of night
"Darling nephew, maybe you should gouge out your eyes--
The war's been lost and everyone died."
Perhaps I should burn the the house down
Reduce it and the box to embers
And then run naked down the street
Covering in soot, yelling at no one "return to sender"

PARCEL THE

Nearsighted Girl in a Polo Shirt #4

The birds of nowhere are on the wire
They carouse slowly in the smoke
Smell the world burning
The gray changing patterns as its turning
Drifting through the days in a haze
Open yourself, see what you've been missin'
Drifting through the days in a haze
Like you've been listening to the Eagles in prison

I liked what her shirt said
Oh, I really liked her smile
I tried to come up with more words for her
But was embarrassed by my guile
I remember someone like her
She had this beauty inside
I remember someone like her
With love in her eyes

When you hang yourself from the tree of anger
You only provide the ones you hate more shade
Shadows like a Rorschach test
Come on down from the gallows and give us all a rest
Oh, but when you burn like that
With the angry side of desire
If I get too close to your fury and smoke
I might be consumed by fire
I liked what her shirt said (etc.)

Magnificent crotch drawings
Pinned up in your grandma's lodge
You try to be cool as cats
But then the world goes to the dogs
Hear the amateur ones howling
More than a little out of key
You get old you learn about the heart
That it is never to be given lightly

I liked what her shirt said
She, I don't know, just seemed kind
But I kept my mouth closed, walked away
And made an art out of losing my mind
I remember someone like her
She had this beauty inside
I remember someone like her
With love in her eyes

nearsighted girl in a polo shirt #4

Play   the Numbers

The weather is strange
Isn't it usually hot by May?
Looking for patterns in the clouds
Over our shoulders so heavy and gray
Got to keep occupied
Like a country without a scheme
Got to keep quite occupied
Life stills like movies or dreams
Play the numbers
Maybe you'll just beat the odds
Go on and play the numbers
Stop being so blonde

These feelings are strange
Like a different life passing by
So much unexplained
Dreaming of things we'd buy
Got to keep occupied
Like a woman with a bad man
Got to keep occupied
Reaching for things we can't understand
Play the numbers
All the lines on your palm
Go on and play the numbers
Maybe life's a mystery we aren't meant to solve
Play the numbers
Your smile is one twist from a sigh
Play the numbers

This is my message so now you reply...

www.ingramcontent.com/pod-product-compliance
Lightning Source LLC
Chambersburg PA
CBHW060444040426
42331CB00044B/2597